In the Furnace *of* Doubts

In the
Furnace of Doubts

Meditations—when you've lost your answers

Catherine de Hueck Doherty

MADONNA HOUSE PUBLICATIONS
Combermere, Ontario, Canada

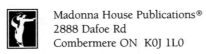

Madonna House Publications®
2888 Dafoe Rd
Combermere ON K0J 1L0

www.madonnahouse.org/publications

© 2002 Madonna House Publications. All rights reserved.

First Edition

First printing, July 16, 2002 — feast of Our Lady of Mount Carmel

Printed in Canada

Scripture quotations are taken from the New Jerusalem Bible, copyright © 1985 by Darton, Longman & Todd, London, and Doubleday, a division of Random House, Inc., New York.

Edited by Martin Nagy. Parts of this work previously appeared in the book *Doubts, Loneliness, Rejection* by Catherine Doherty, which was published by Madonna House Publications in 1993.

National Library of Canada Cataloguing in Publication Data

Doherty, Catherine de Hueck (née Kolyschkine), 1896–1985
  In the furnace of doubts : meditations—when you've lost your answers

ISBN 0-921440-80-4

  1. Faith—Meditations. 2. Belief and doubt—Meditations. I. Title.

BT771.3.D63 2002   242'.72   C2002-902814-0

Design by Rob Huston

This book is set in Berkeley Oldstyle, designed by Frederick W. Goudy for the University of California Press in 1938. Headings are set in Balzano, designed by America's famous carver of inscriptions, John Benson.

It was not as a child that I learned
to believe in Christ and confess his faith.
My Hosanna has burst forth
from a huge furnace of doubt.

Fyodor Dostoevsky

My child, if you aspire to serve the Lord,
prepare yourself for an ordeal...
Whatever happens to you, accept it,
and in the uncertainties
of your humble state, be patient,
since gold is tested in the fire,
and the chosen
in the furnace of humiliation.

Ecclesiasticus 2:1,4–5

Contents

Introduction

Faith is given to us, in baptism, by God himself, but we are supposed to make it grow, and we do. Yet, quite unexpectedly, the tree of faith which seemed to be so strong, suddenly looks spindly and weak.

At that moment, we face our greatest enemy and, at the same time, perhaps our greatest friend. We face doubt. Doubt of God's existence. Doubt of his goodness. Doubt of his power. Doubt of everything connected with him and about him. But this doubt draws us closer to him. Those who doubt, cry out to him. And he comes.

At this moment, remember the apostle, St. Thomas. If he did not have doubts, I might not have the courage to doubt either. I might know Christ in an entirely different way. Reading about the doubts of Thomas brought me a knowledge of God that I didn't possess before:

"Thomas, called the Twin, who was one of the Twelve, was not with them when Jesus came. So the other disciples said to him, 'We have seen the Lord,' but he answered,

'Unless I can see the holes that the nails made in his hands and can put my finger into the holes they made, and unless I can put my hand into his side, I refuse to believe.'

"Eight days later the disciples were in the house again and Thomas was with them. The doors were closed, but Jesus came in and stood among them. 'Peace be with you,' he said. Then he spoke to Thomas, 'Put your finger here; look, here are my hands. Give me your hand; put it into my side. Do not be unbelieving any more but believe.'

"Thomas replied, 'My Lord and my God!'

"Jesus said to him:

'You believe because you can see me. Blessed are those who have not seen and yet believe.'" (John 20:24–29)

We are about to meditate and pray through a malady of our age. Perhaps the virus of doubts began long ago, but it has come to full maturity. Man is confronted with himself; alone he faces his doubts. Sometimes he cannot take it, and he shares it with someone else—a priest, a fellow worker, a spouse, a girlfriend.

Through these meditations on doubts, which incidentally came to me in the dark hours of the night, it seemed as if the Lord was saying, "Write about their doubts, because everybody doubts everything and everyone today, especially my Father, me, and the Holy Spirit." Yes, this is the hour, then, of shedding our doubts. This is the hour of prayer. Doubts are silenced only by prayer. You will be surprised how small they are. They're like little chestnuts, falling in autumn, crushed underfoot by faith. They really do not matter at all.

Miraculously, man knows that he cannot doubt any more. He believes with his whole heart in the Triune God and in Our Lady and in all of the Church's teaching. *He believes that in them is hidden the answer to all doubts.* By belief, we become people of faith, people of Christ.

Does God Exist?

"Ask, and it will be given to you; search, and you will find; knock, and the door will be opened to you. Everyone who asks receives; everyone who searches finds; everyone who knocks will have the door opened. Is there anyone among you who would hand his son a stone when he asked for bread? Or would hand him a snake when he asked for a fish? If you, then, evil as you are, know how to give your children what is good, how much more will your Father in heaven give good things to those who ask him!"

Matthew 7:7–11

Keep Digging

There are very few people living who haven't doubted the existence of God. I must confess. I did.

Doubt is a strange thing. It comes unbidden, unexpectedly, suddenly. Or, it can come slowly, entering the intellect and playing havoc with it, in a matter of speaking, so that the intellect for a moment or two, suddenly, truly, does not believe in God. Yet, this strange earth that has been plowed and harrowed for a thousand years is the very earth from which faith springs. A very strange and contradictory thought.

The moment when I or you have really made up our minds that God is a mystery, then, out of the strange earth that has been worked so much, so long, so hard, comes faith.

Doubt Your Doubts

So you begin to have doubts—a very wholesome occupation. To have doubts really brings one closer to God, for he expected and expects to be doubted. In fact, while he was on earth, his miracles and all his speeches were directed to people who obviously doubted what he said.

Take, for instance, when he said: "In all truth I tell you, if you do not eat the flesh of the Son of Man and drink his blood, you have no life in you." (John 6:53) The Jews left him, as many did. Then, he turned around to the apostles and said, "What about you, do you want to go away too?" (John 6:67) That was the moment of faith.

In harboring doubts you understand something you didn't understand before, and the mystery of Christ opens its doors to you. I have a suspicion that it is the doubter who knocks at the door of Christ. The "righteous one" who never doubts, doesn't knock at God's heart. Only those who doubt cry out to him. Return and knock at his heart. At once the heart opens, the doubts vanish, and, for a while, all is well.

Cry out to Jesus. Return and knock at his heart.

Put Your Trust in God Because People Will Disappoint You

"Remind them of this; and tell them in the name of God that there must be no wrangling about words: all that this ever achieves is the destruction of those who are listening. Make every effort to present yourself before God as a proven worker who has no need to be ashamed, but who keeps the message of truth on a straight path."

2 Timothy 2:14,15

Ashes

We lay out on a table, like a picture puzzle, the pieces of doubt that we have about God. We examine them separately and we try to fit one into the other. Seldom does anything fit, but anyhow, we try. And so, because we are "in doubt," or so we think, we let him fall out of our lives. I think when you let God fall, the world shakes.

Still, here before me are all the doubts I ever had toward God. They are strange picture puzzles. They grow little roots and tie themselves to the place of their origin, and they don't want to go away. You have to pull at them and throw them into the fire, for all of our doubts apply to God. They turn to ashes no matter how clever, how brilliant, how fantastic we are.

Sift Through the Facts and the Doubts

When you think of Engels, who was the teacher of Marx, and of Marx who implemented the teaching of Engels, what have you got? Marx attributed to religion a thousand evils, and he was right about many of them. There were doubts and there were facts. We have to be very careful in sifting our facts and doubts.

To give you an example, as far as you are concerned, your parish's pastor is not up to your expectations. He barely celebrates Mass decently. His manner of hearing Confession doesn't appeal to you. These may be facts about his given traits, but that doesn't mean that you doubt all priests. And even in regard to your pastor, you have the faith that tells you that Christ lives in him.

Face Your Doubts

Here on one side is a doubt, because papa, mama, a priest, or authority of any kind has let you down, or so you think. But is all authority like that? All of us doubt at one time or another. But we must burn our doubts in a firey holocaust, because we know that our doubts are only phantoms.

It is good for us to go into a chapel, or any place, sit down in the evening quietly, and face our doubts one by one, and realize that the road of doubts is the road to perdition. It can lead only to a hell of our own making.

I should be the first to tell you this, for to bring forth an apostolate like Madonna House, in the beginning, I doubted at every step. Only the burning of doubts and the growth of faith, which go together, can achieve an apostolate. Squabbles inside, squabbles outside, being denounced by priests, disliked by bishops, ridiculed by Black leaders, ridiculed by organized labor, ridiculed by your own, I was lying there somewhere on a pavement, all bruised and battered. Doubts, new and old, came forth and touched me like a soft kitten's paw.

Doubts are around all the time—throw them into the fire, the fire of God's love. When you love him you believe in him. When you believe in him and love him, you hope. Faith, love, and hope sweep away doubts. Try it some time.

Throw your doubts into the fire of God's love. Love him. Believe him. Sweep away your doubts through faith, hope, and love.

When You Feel Like Giving Up

"One thing I ask of Yahweh,
one thing I seek:
to dwell in Yahweh's house
all the days of my life,
to enjoy the sweetness of Yahweh,
to seek out his temple."

Psalm 27:4

You Have to Get Up and Keep Going

It is time to get up. I don't want to get up. Frankly, I want to die. My little room in Harlem contains many things—a refrigerator that doesn't work, a gas stove that does, a big sink that is like a laundry sink, a lamp in the middle of the ceiling swaying a little if there is a breeze in summer. Alas, there is really very little breeze in my room.

But it is time to get up!

Slowly I do. Oh, I have a bathroom attached to my room. But in winter I use the water sparingly to wash myself, because the water is very cold. It refreshes me for a little while. I dress and I contemplate breakfast, which I shouldn't do because I have to go to Mass.

Keep Praying Anyway

Slowly and reluctantly, I go. I lock the door with several locks, as you always do in places where the poor live. I cross the street and there is the church. I walk into it, trying to avoid what appears to me to be a thousand children playing on the street. There are not enough streets set aside for children to play. And the air is polluted, not only from exhausts, but from all the smells that come from the East River.

But I guess I am used to it. I make my way through the children who greet me. According to the kids, if I pray to the Holy Spirit, he will give them the things that they want—namely, baseball bats and a ball and such. I doubt my prayer. Mostly, it is the goodness of the Knights of Columbus and other organizations who provide the bats and balls, not me.

Find Refuge in the Church

I enter the dim church. There are very few people. It looks deserted, or almost so. I look at the statue of Saint Martin de Porres on the right and Our Lady on the left side. In the middle, the priest offers Mass. I am just in time.

There are about five people in that big church. I kneel down and try to shake from me the terrible darkness that holds me tight, but I don't seem to be able to do so.

Snatches of the Gospel, and of the Old Testament, keep coming vividly to my mind.

I do not want to leave the church. It is like a refuge of some sort, almost an escape. The priest is saying Mass. The Body and Blood of Christ is being offered for me as well as for others. This is the time to believe. This is not the time for doubts or for non-surrender, for all the strange emotions that fill my soul.

For the Love of God

I try to concentrate. The voices of the children grow louder than the words of the priest. I try to remember that Christ said to let the children come to him. He seemed not to mind their stridency, their questions, their bothering him. You know how children are. They pull at your garment when they want your attention. They yell in one ear and whisper in another. Yes, that's the way of children. Again I find myself praying over so many doubts which occur outside the church door.

The poverty of those people is enough to make one cry. I remember carrying a mattress to an old lady. It was a heavy mattress but I was strong, then. I was doubled up carrying it. Some boys stretched out their legs and I fell over them. I bruised myself. They were the very poor whom I had come to serve. Everything in me rebelled. Everything in me cried out, "Take the next train tonight and go back to Canada of the tall pines and the limpid waters."

Yes, I was shaken by doubts. Have you ever been shaken by doubts so that you wondered why you were even in a church? Well, that's the way I was.

Find Refreshment in the Eucharist

Then, seemingly from a very great distance, almost as if from across a desert, the words, "Take and eat, this is My Body" came to me. And, from much closer, I clearly heard, "This is My Blood, the Blood of the new covenant, which is poured out for many for the forgiveness of sins."

I walked up to the altar railing, I opened my mouth, and received my Love. Suddenly, everything was changed. The church seemed filled with a lovely light, and I returned to my place. The voices of the children stopped being strident and became joyous, like the flowing rivers in Canada.

As I came out of the church I saw them, a big forest of children, just like the forests of Canada, tall and slender. They were all laughing and surrounding me and calling me the "B," and I felt proud and happy because of this appellation. To these children I was the bee that collected things for them, as a bee collects sweetness from all the flowers. My whole apostolate of Friendship House in Harlem suddenly became as sweet as honey from the honeycomb.

Receive the Eucharist and be refreshed. And then go look for sweetness in your situation and those around you.

Why Am I Here?

"This is my commandment:
love one another,
as I have loved you.
No one can have greater love
than to lay down his life for his friends."

John 15:12,13

Surrender to Love

Did you know that doubts sometimes have very quiet feet? I think they sometimes wear flannels on their feet so that no one can hear how they creep into your heart, your mind, your soul.

Bingo, they are gone! Bingo, there they are!

I was surrounded by the poor in Harlem. They were so tragically poor, so handicapped, that my heart wept for them, even as my mind rebelled. As I dressed one day, I was asking myself why I was there. Doubts, like so many poisonous snakes, were filling my mind. What about all those slums? What about God's promises to help the poor?

You know something? I didn't want to surrender. "Surrender" was a very frightening word, and yet it was the word that I thought most about. It came to me in a thousand ways.

When you are in love, you surrender. It's not merely a surrender of your body. That would be lust. You surrender to a man or woman because you love him or her, and then surrender takes on an entirely different meaning. It is equated with love. Yes, there were moments in my life when I knew that surrender was love.

The Crucifix

How did I know that? That's very simple. I looked at the crucifix. Sometimes I averted my eyes from the crucifix because it was a symbol of surrender. I started thinking straight, instead of thinking crookedly. God became man. That was some surrender.

God, the second person of the Holy Trinity, became human to save us. Think about it. When doubts assail you like a thousand flies buzzing in your ears and heart and mind and all around you, think about God becoming a human person.

He was obedient to his parents; he was obedient unto death to his Father in heaven. Think about that, and lay all your doubts before that obedience. Then, you will understand what the word "surrender" means.

Don't stop. Go a little further. Now he is being crucified. Can you hear nails against wood? Those are the sounds that the doubters hear at night. Nails against wood. He died for us because he loved us. So, it is obvious that surrender means love. Do we love? Now that, my friend, is the question. The answer is, "very little," or we wouldn't have wars or all the tragedies that we are surrounded with.

Love means open arms ready to embrace you. That's what Christ did when he was crucified.

Think again, and get to the bottom of the word surrender. You will find that it has no bottom.

Life Is Monotonous

"Let everything you do be done in love."

1 Corinthians 16:14

Life Is Nitty-Gritty

Life goes on its way. Actually, life is really a nitty-gritty affair. Whatever we happen to be doing, life is fundamentally repetitious. Are we looking after babies or children? It's monotonous—washing diapers, dressing babies, putting them to bed, feeding them, entertaining them the best you can. Day after day, it gets monotonous, doesn't it?

So many women find home monotonous. The daily chores, if taken all together, are monotonous. Cooking, scrubbing, washing. No matter how modern machines may seem to take the monotony out of it, it still gets monotonous. We don't know what to do with ourselves sometimes—most of the time. When the washing machine goes zip, zip, and the dishwasher goes bloop, bloop, it seems monotonous.

Doubts sometimes have noisy feet that stomp around in our monotony demanding attention. They have the key to every human heart. Men and women feel the monotony of nitty-gritty daily living. I am sure that even the President finds a certain monotony to his job from which he would like to escape by jogging, and sometimes does, or by skiing on the other side of the country. Sign papers, meet the Congress, don't meet the Congress, be here at this time, be there another time. It can be just as monotonous as anything else. From the Presidency to manual labor, monotony can become the path of doubts. Time must be filled somehow. And so husband, wife, and children, all feel the weight of this monotony, of this sameness, of this nitty-gritty, daily doubt.

Wanting to Rebel against the Nitty-Gritty

Stop for a moment and think of the daily life of millions of people, from India to Europe, from Europe to the Sahara Desert. Just stop and think how monotonous it is and how easily doubts can penetrate.

Doubts can come openly. They screech within our hearts. It is not a question of being quiet, of pondering something in the depths of your heart. No. It is the rebellion that one feels against the nitty-gritty of daily life.

When we are young, we dream our dreams. We are going to change the world. We are going to do this, and we are going to do that. Yes, all those things we are going to do. But the years go by. We become book-keepers or sales clerks. Our job is monotonous, and we are assailed by all kinds of thoughts. The nitty-gritty, daily life of people is the widest road to doubts.

God has given us a small road, a small path, and has bidden us to follow him no matter what, but we can't. And just around the corner lies the path that is wide, covered with blacktop, bordered by trimmed trees and permeated with a pleasant air. Our own path is full of doubts. We feel that if only we could pass a little divide, let's say a little river that has a bridge that would help us. If only we did that, we would renew ourselves. We would get rid of all those doubts and we would be free. So there we stand, in front of a bridge, or maybe just another path, that leads directly onto that wide blacktop road, beside which the flowers are scented and the pine trees grow tall.

We hesitate. Our lives are dreary, so we think. We stare at the bridge, feeling that there is nothing new in our lives.

We've Forgotten; We've Become Unaware

Doing our daily chores isn't really monotonous, it doesn't need to feel monotonous, because one's own child is full of surprises and provides surprises for father and mother. We forget the smile of a child which we suddenly caught and which made us smile in return. We are totally unaware of children calling us to come and play with them. We are too occupied with our ideas to respond to their calls. Youth passes by, filled with questions that it wants answered. We are supposed to be the ones to answer them, but we are so preoccupied with that little bridge and big blacktop road, that we let them pass by.

We are about to put our foot on that bridge when we casually glance at an old woman sitting by the bridge. She knows all the answers, but we do not stop to find out what she knows. We are going to cross the bridge and find out for ourselves; so we do.

The average day of man, woman, and child, appears to be very dull. Even a child has doubts. He has doubts because his elders doubt. A child is so sensitive that he or she responds to the kind of atmosphere fashioned by the adult.

There we are. We're walking on the straight blacktop road, now. A strange thing happens. The lovely smell of flowers that attracted us from the other side has vanished, is vanishing more and more. We turn the corner, and their perfume goes away completely, and we are filled with doubts again.

Doubts about our life. We wonder, what are we doing on this earth? Thousands of people will die today, maybe millions, and these people will never know our search. They will go on the wide blacktop road, and they will find there emptiness. Emptiness. That's where the beautiful blacktop road leads—to complete emptiness.

It is not just a question of doubts. We know that as we travel on that road, it will become empty. With every step that we make, we lose something. What it is that we lose we won't know this side of heaven. But one thing we will know. Each time we take that step, we lose the clear image of God, until finally he seems not to exist any more. There we are, surrounded by all our doubts. Then, strange as it might seem, our doubts alone reflect the face of God.

Fall in Love

All feel the weight of this monotony, that is, if they are not in love with God. When they're in love, the monotonous moments, the doubts are not so powerful nor so devastating.

There is something that can yet be straightened out if we get off the blacktop road and onto the little path that God has given us to walk on. If we do, we will know that that little path is holy. We'll catch the smile of a child in both our hands and hug it to our heart. We'll answer the call of young ones to come and play, and we will answer the questions of those children who are a little older.

All the nitty-gritty days that seemed so monotonous, so full of temptations and doubts, will vanish, and we'll walk barefoot as pilgrims do, down a strange path from which flowers will sprout. Trees will grow around about it, and we'll understand that this is the path that God has made, and there is nothing nitty-gritty about it. And everything about it is exciting, because we will be in love with God. And to be in love with God is the most exciting thing in the world.

Be in love with God, because to be in love with God is the most exciting thing in the world.

Terror and War

"Though an army pitch camp against me,
my heart will not fear,
though war break out against me,
my trust will never be shaken...
For he hides me away under his roof
on the day of evil,
he folds me in the recesses of his tent,
sets me high on a rock.
Put your hope in Yahweh, be strong,
let your heart be bold,
put your hope in Yahweh."

Psalm 27:3,5,14

I Cannot Understand War

I stand in the middle of our path here and repeat, parrot-like, "Lord have mercy, Christ have mercy, Lord have mercy." I really don't think of what I am saying. I am surrounded. There is a war on. Doubts assail me. Doubts in the mercy of God, in his goodness, and even in his ability to stop the war. I look at these dancing figures that are so horrible, and I know that I doubt, I doubt deeply and profoundly. I cannot understand.

Why should those young people be killed in their youth, or maimed? I ask God loudly and clearly, "Why?" and the echo brings my why back to me. I am shaken as I see wounded people in front of me, shaken as with a fever.

Is God Not True to His Promise?

All around me lie the bones of my doubts. God who promised to look after the poor, the sick, the lonely, seems false to his promise. How can it be? God cannot be false to anything, because he is God. And suddenly I find my face wet with tears. I am encircled with those doubts. They come closer and closer and closer. It is as if at any minute I shall die in the arms of my doubts. Have you ever felt that way? Have you doubted when great catastrophes befell your country? On the people that you love? Have you doubted?

I did. It would be a lie to say that I didn't. I really doubted the very existence of God. And right in the midst of my doubt, I was lifted up, high above all clouds, above all doubts, above all tragedies, and I nestled myself between the wings of the Crimson Dove, the Holy Spirit, and a great peace came upon me.

I understood that we were the ones who brought about the wounding of our soldiers, by entering into another war. We always enter into another war. It is our will that does it, not God's. The torture of my doubts falls away from me. I nestle in the Holy Spirit's wings like a child nestles in his mother's arms, and all is peace.

Nestle in the Holy Spirit's wings like a child nestles in his mother's arms and find peace.

Emptiness

*"Even were I to walk in a ravine as dark as death
I should fear no danger, for you are at my side."*

Psalm 23:4

Have You Felt an Emptiness
Taking Hold of You?

Did you ever feel as if the earth were moving under your feet? Not you walking over it, but it moving under you. Fast, fast, fast, so fast that you could not catch up to it with your own feet. Did you ever feel that way?

Did you ever feel as if life were not worth living? Did you feel the days following days in that kind of monotony, a monotony that becomes unbearable?

Did you ever stand still and suddenly feel besieged by every doubt that ever surrounded man? Did you ever see yourself as a skeleton reposing in the earth, slowly disappearing into the dust and while you were lying there, hearing the words "Dust unto dust"?

Have you ever sat quietly in your room all by yourself, watching the sunset fade away, and reiterated the doubts that you had about God? "Does God exist? . . . If so, why doesn't he manifest himself? . . . Not necessarily in miracles, but in the truths that were enunciated in the Old Testament and the gospels . . ." Did you feel at such moments a total emptiness taking hold of you?

Walk into the Darkness

Many doubts are assailing you, but you can't shoo them away. They swarm around you like flies on a sunny afternoon. Perhaps you haven't got the strength to lift the fly swatter. Maybe that's it. Or maybe you just don't care. All these things do happen to people. There are people who believed and hoped and loved, yet, at particular moments, love, hope, and faith disappear.

Nothing remains except a darkness—a frightening, diabolical darkness. You stand before that curtain of darkness, and ask yourself, "Do I have the courage to enter?" All around you a thousand noises, a thousand voices whisper, "No, no, no, stay in the light." But something that you cannot put your finger on, something that is almost phantom-like in the depths of your soul and in the depths of your heart, makes you walk.

Then, it isn't the earth that is moving too fast for you. No, you walk into the darkness like a soldier walks into battle. You walk with fear in your heart. It is said of fear that it exists to be overcome, and so you overcome it in this diabolical darkness. You walk, and on the first step you already know that faith is yours. You plow on. You plow on like a plow against the earth. But you plow not against the earth, but against your fears.

Keep Walking

And slowly you see your fears overcome, you see them all collapse. You stand before this curtain, this dark diabolical black curtain, and you remember that you cannot be afraid. You have to walk into this darkness. For when you walk into it, you will find him whom you love. But you are not yet aware of that.

You make the first step, the second step, the third step, and behold, fear falls from you like a mantle. See, over there in that corner, fear went there and then disappeared. You overcame it, and now dawn is showing through.

And suddenly there is no more darkness. There is faith, there is love, there is hope, and there somewhere, far down the road, is a person. You cannot see from afar if it is a man, a woman, or a child, but you run towards the person, because now you know you have passed the curtain of a thousand doubts.

At the end of those thousand doubts, at the end of your emptiness lies nothing but faith, love, and hope. Keep walking. Plow on through your doubts.

When You Are Anxious

*"Can anything cut us off from the love of Christ—
can hardships or distress, or persecution, or lack of
food and clothing, or threats or violence...*

*No; we come through all these things tri-
umphantly victorious, by the power of him who loved
us. For I am certain of this: neither death nor life,
nor angels, nor principalities, nothing already in
existence and nothing still to come, nor any power,
nor the heights nor the depths, nor any created thing
whatever, will be able to come between us and the
love of God, known to us in Christ Jesus our Lord."*

Romans 8:35,37–39

We Are Afraid of Many Things

We are afraid of so many things, and most of
the time fear holds us tight. Fear is to be
overcome, because once fear is overcome,
hosts of its attendants disappear. Fear of
people, fear of involvement, fear of our-

selves, and an endless sea of doubts about our security, about our identity, and so on. We face fear over and over again under new guises.

But how do we overcome fear? First and foremost, by prayer. Fear is overcome by courage, too. Courage is not the absence of fear, it is the overcoming of it.

What are we afraid of? Pause for a moment and consider this question.

What Are We Really Afraid Of?

Above all, we are afraid of death, of that strange annihilation that occurs to all of us. Death is the crux of our fears. The brain that functions so well, that talent that was so great, that scientific knowledge that helped humanity in so many ways, all will suddenly cease to exist. Other fears beset our life, but the fear of death is the real fear.

Let's examine this. The fear of death is surrounded by doubts. Death is the center of doubt. We are afraid of dying, even in our youth. This fear places in our lap all of our doubts about the existence of God. In the face of this fear, we wonder, "Where is God?" From this question, one of the deepest doubts begins to fill our hearts, "Does God exist?"

The majority stop right here and try to forget what they cannot ever forget.

Others go deeper. They ask the same question, "Does God exist?" but they want to separate it from the idea of dying. They want to prove to themselves that they are not afraid of death. Since they doubt God's existence, though, a whole series of objections arise in their hearts: "He is absent." "He is not there when needed." "He inflicts pain most of the time." "To serve him is foolishness because serving him means an identification with him." And who wants to be identified with Christ, for Christ always, I repeat, always brings pain.

The essence, then, or center of our fears is death. Fear of death is the root fear, and we might as well face it. It is *the* radical fear and the reason for all fears.

Why Are We Afraid of Death?

But why should we be afraid of death? Death is one of the most beautiful moments of life. If one has faith, the entry into death is a glorious one. It is not a question of seeing angels or Our Lady. It really means being greeted by Christ himself, of being invaded by his life, being one with him. Christ has conquered death. Death is our passage into an eternity with him.

Remember daily that you will die. But also remember that dying is a joyful event. God will greet God in you. You will be one with Christ.

Feeling on the Verge of Catastrophe

"You fence me in, behind and in front,
you have laid your hand upon me...
Where shall I go to escape your spirit?
Where shall I flee from your presence?
...If I speed away on the wings of the dawn,
if I dwell beyond the ocean,
even there your hand will be guiding me,
your right hand holding me fast...
You created my inmost self,
knit me together in my mother's womb...
Your eyes could see my embryo.
In your book all my days were inscribed,
every one that was fixed is there...
God, examine me and know my heart,
test me and know my concerns.
Make sure that I am not on my way to ruin,
and guide me on the road of eternity."

Psalm 139:5,7,9–10,13,16,23–24

Doubts Assail Us Because We Love God

News of war and rumors of new wars are cast about by the media like birds of ill omen. We are in the midst of doubt. There is no getting away from it. The radio blares; the TV blares. There is the massing of the troops on borders. The arms race accelerates. How is it possible not to doubt? Are there any around us who do not doubt?

I know that I doubt, and yet I love God beyond all loves. Doubts assail you, too, because you are in love with God.

Doubts Come From the Hell We Create

Doubts come from fear, but they also come from the depths of human hell, the hell that man creates within his own heart.

Doubts gnaw at me like quiet little mice eating up the cheese of my soul, of my mind, of my heart. I turn around, and I don't know any more where I am. Doubts have almost conquered me. To contemplate the troubles of our nation, to worry about them, is not easy for anyone, but that is where our imagination takes us.

Doubts and fears assail us: many manufacturers have put their lights out; businesses and factories are closing. There is a fault in the earth that might, even tomorrow, bring about one of the most terrible earthquakes that we have ever seen or heard of, bigger than the earthquake in San Francisco in the early 1900s, in cities that have grown larger in population.

I am afraid to go in a plane. I am afraid to go on a train. I am afraid to go in a bus. There are so many that collide, so many accidents with planes and trains and cars.

And the water isn't safe. There is pollution all over the place.

As I sit here, doubts seem to have become a part of me. Truly, I look at the world and I think, is it worth living in this world? Doubts shake me, doubts about the existence of God, his benevolence, his tenderness, his love, his goodness. All seem to have disappeared suddenly in some kind of a green ocean, and I am moving into it.

You Belong to God

I enter the water without the proper diving suit. Waves hit me in the face. Am I drowning because I ceased to believe? Is that why I am in this green depth? But when it seems to me that all is finished, I am suddenly lifted up. I am lifted up and a voice out of the green depths, out of the blue-green of the sea, tells me:

"This day I have begotten you. I have thought about you before you entered your mother's womb. You belong to me. I am your God. I am your Father. I am your Lover. I am your Spirit. You have been in my mind for all eternity. I have begotten you. Into your mother's womb I have placed you, from her I have received you into my arms. I have loved you, and I have prepared a place for you in which you will be with me and my Son and the Holy Spirit, and where Our Lady will teach you the immense joy of being a Christian."

At the words of our Lord, the green depths vanish. Everything vanishes. Only the tenderness of God remains, and the doubts vanish as if they had never been.

Desolation and Destruction

"Yahweh is near to the broken-hearted,
he helps those whose spirit is crushed.
Though hardships without number beset the upright,
Yahweh brings rescue from them all."

Psalm 34:18–19

The Anxiety of Facing Horrific Desolation

When I think of World War I, when I think
of starvation in Russia, when I think of
escapes to foreign lands at the risk of one's
life, when I think of being present at the
beginning of the Hitler horror, when I think
of Spain and all I saw there, the abomination
of desolation takes hold of me, and I stand
still.

I remember. I remember standing still
because there was nowhere to go mentally,

intellectually, or emotionally. Facing horrific desolation, this abomination vomits its doubts into your heart as it did into mine. I cried out, silently, because I couldn't bear to hear my own voice. I cried out silently to God, "Where are you? What has happened to you? Where have you disappeared to?"

Stand Still

Surrounded by doubts that were deep and profound, I ceased to cry. The doubts about the existence of God, about his having abandoned us, left me. Even though all around me there were Russian refugees—close to twelve million of us, and we were only the first ones—the doubts ceased.

Yes, where was God? Anyone who has gone through that abomination of desolation knows what I mean. There are so many refugees these days that they must know, without my writing about it, what it is all about.

Slowly, faith reasserted itself, and out of that abomination, out of that desolation, came the knowledge that to follow Christ means to walk constantly in pain and in joy.

Today too, doubts come creeping slowly into one's mind, like rodents seemingly busy about eating up our brains. For we are confronted today with terror, with nuclear weapons, with weapons of mass destruction. Doubts, like rodents with sharp teeth, seem to eat away at us, without eating us up all at once as perhaps a lion would; but only a little here, a little there, each bite being a doubt, a doubt in the very existence of God.

It is not a question of accidentals. No, this time the very depths of our faith are being corroded, are being eaten up. There are so many doubts and so few answers. The answers are few because faith must give the answer. Faith surpasses reason, logic, and all the other things that man prides himself on.

Wait for God

And so, in the midst of an abomination of desolation, we stand in a strange sort of middle. On the one side, faith; on the other side, doubts. Doubts seem to overwhelm faith.

This is a strange moment. It's really a crucial moment, for those who believe. Once more, Christians are tested individually. The abomination of desolation is slowly creeping upon us, and with it, doubts. At this moment, when everything seems to crumble within the self, an almost suicidal desire comes upon you. To give in to doubts, to forget all that we call faith, to live a life that is exclusively one's own and has no relation to God, this is not the way.

Suddenly, out of the fog, comes a woman, wrapped in silence. She holds out her hands to you. You put your hands into her hands, she opens the big, beautiful mantle of silence that she is wrapped in. And she wraps you in it herself. At that very moment, even though the abomination of desolation might be all around you, as the mantle touches you, all doubts disappear. The desolation might not disappear because men bring it about themselves, but the doubts disappear.

When you are wrapped in the mantle of the woman who herself is wrapped in silence, when you allow yourself to be wrapped up in the silence of the Mother of God, your doubts, too, are silenced.

God is Found Through Doubts

"Let him test me in the crucible:
I shall come out pure gold."

Job 23:10

The Doubts Are Unbearable

Sometimes, the moments of doubt against God, against the Trinity, the angels, the saints, become unbearable. It is as if you had descended into some kind of a pit from which you look upward and you see only darkness. There is no light any more. There is nothing to hold you up. You sit on a knoll and you look into the darkness, and in your heart you ask yourself the question men have asked themselves for an eternity, "Where is God?"

Especially now that we have spacecraft that can circle the planets and send back to us all kinds of photographs to show us that apparently there is no human life anywhere in this solar system, you consider what you know from the scientific point of view, and you say to yourself, "Where is God? On what planet?"

Then a modicum of sense comes back to you, and you say, "Well, God is not on any planet." You knew that anyhow. He is in you, within that strange place called "spirit." And you recall all that scientists have discovered about the human brain.

I knew a doctor whose specialty was brain surgery; he was a believer, a Catholic. He used an electrical instrument to make a chart of the brain. There was one part of the brain which showed activity whenever the person being charted began speaking of God. It was a spiritual place. The doctor never said anything, he just marked that this was the spot. Think about that as you look upwards when you feel nothing but black darkness.

A Tree Grows in the Darkness

You just read some place that they discovered a skeleton that was twenty million years old. You say to yourself, "*This* is going to come alive and resurrect as the gospel says?" Then, for some unaccountable reason, you begin to weep. It's as if all your dreams were shattered, as if death was really the end. And there you are, sitting on your knoll, doubting again.

You have a flashlight. In your darkness, you use the flashlight and you read the Psalms or the breviary, and you read that God is going to do this and that for the Jews, and he's going to shelter the poor and so forth. Then you look at your past history when you tried to bring pity and tenderness and food to the slums. And you wonder again.

Then suddenly, it is as if everything dissolves and there is nothing. Now doubts have really mastered you. You are not sitting on that knoll, you are lying on it, and somebody is beating you to a pulp. Haven't you ever felt that way?

Then, out of the darkness a tree comes forth, a very small tree. And while you're being beaten black and blue by your doubts, the tree grows faster than your beatings. Suddenly, nobody is beating you. You are just lying under the immense branches of a beautiful tree.

You know, almost without knowing, that it isn't growing on the knoll or in some soil around you. It's growing from your heart. You lift your eyes, and you are confronted with God himself. He says, "You have passed another Rubicon. You have allowed doubts to besiege you. It's through doubt that you find me. Those who do not doubt, do not find me."

Through doubt you find God. Your doubts lead you home. Those who do not go through doubts, do not find God.

God's Grace Is Enough

"He has answered me, 'My grace is enough for you: for power is at full stretch in weakness.' It is, then, about my weaknesses that I am happiest of all to boast, so that the power of Christ may rest upon me; and that is why I am glad of weaknesses, insults, constraints, persecutions and distress for Christ's sake. For it is when I am weak that I am strong."

2 Corinthians 12:9–10

The Pilgrimage

That is what the Lord said to me, "Those who do not doubt, do not find me."

It's a very strange sentence, is it not? But at the same time, it's very true. Those who do not doubt are not on a pilgrimage. You can, indeed, believe in God, superficially; but those who seek him, who really want to find the Absolute, as he is, go on a pilgrimage.

It should be a very simple pilgrimage, because the way to find God is in the other person. There is some strange kind of mystery in all this. Why trust in one person would open immense horizons of love and trust is truly a mystery.

Prostrate Yourself before a Mystery

You should kneel before a mystery, and sometimes, even prostrate yourself before mysteries. Only God can reveal them to you or to me, and then, in a quite mysterious way. As far as we're concerned, he decrees that whatever we do to the least of his brethren, we do to him. Pause to think about that.

The Key to Trusting God

When we enter the desert of doubts, let us stoop and pause and understand that we are on a pilgrimage. This moves our souls, our hearts, ever closer, closer, closer to God. And that strange mystery of believing when there is nothing to believe in is the key to a complete trust in God and the dissolution of doubt.

But, of course, we do not have time these days to pray, kneel, and prostrate ourselves—or at least, we think we haven't. And so, doubts assail us from all quarters.

For instance, take war, about which there are so many rumors. We are afraid, and doubts about the power of God are rampant. Frankly, we then have to stop and consider. Our pilgrimage must not go any further because if there is going to be a war, cold or hot, let me assure you, we made it so.

Greed, selfishness, desire for power—these are the motivations which cause both hot and cold wars; and who is guilty of them? Men and women are. They still do not cooperate. They still want to possess for themselves the goods of the earth that God has placed in it—gold, silver, uranium, oil. Men and women do not wish to cooperate. They do not wish to love one another.

Once again, Christ is crying out, "I give you a new commandment: love one another; you must love one another just as I have loved you." (John 13: 34) Christ is offering peace, joy, love, hope, all things we hunger for, and we disregard them in order to make our factories work and our cars run.

Doubt Yourself

If instead of doubting God, we doubted ourselves, we could begin a new style of life with small farms, with love for one another, with no desire for power, no lust for acquiring gold and silver. If this would happen, then we would trust God. But it isn't happening, and my soul in agony cries out to God, "From the depths I call to you, Yahweh: Lord, hear my cry. Listen attentively to the sound of my pleading!" (Psalm 130:1,2)

Oh, if only we would permit his infinite grace to inundate our hearts totally, completely, we would sleep in peace once again and awake refreshed, believers. There would be no more doubts. If only we would go into a sleep to the tune of Our Lady's lullaby, after we woke up, lo and behold, there would be no doubts.

Prostrate yourself before God, and let his infinite grace inundate your heart.

The Devil
is the Sower of Doubt

"Bow down, then, before the power of God now, so that he may raise you up in due time; unload all your burden on to him, since he is concerned about you. Keep sober and alert, because your enemy the devil is on the prowl like a roaring lion, looking for someone to devour. Stand up to him, strong in faith and in the knowledge that it is the same kind of suffering that the community of your brothers throughout the world is undergoing. You will have to suffer only for a little while: the God of all grace who called you to eternal glory in Christ will restore you, he will confirm, strengthen and support you."

1 Peter 5:6–10

The Father of Doubts

It's amazing what Satan can do. All human beings must have doubts about the existence of God. Many people have begun to recognize that there is a devil. And I think that they're beginning to know that he, to a great extent, is the sower of their doubts.

I confess that there are lots of doubts that are not directly begotten by the evil one, but fundamentally they all stem from him. He is the father of doubts, for he wanted to be like God. But he was thwarted in his desire. This might seem very old-fashioned to some. I can picture some still ridiculing this.

Nonetheless, in his heart, the evil one begets doubts, and each one of them he sends forth to humanity, so that human beings will doubt, and especially in a way that will separate them from God.

It is true that, unless you doubt God, you will not find him. We start on a pilgrimage filled with high ideals, and after long, weary miles we begin to wonder why we undertook this pilgrimage. Doubts assail us on every side, and temptations, too, for the evil one is not content to sow doubts in our mind. He wants us to follow the path of evil, the path to denial of God. He has succeeded all too well, lately, hasn't he?

Prayer, Fasting, and Obedience

We see the agony of priests who leave the priesthood, of nuns who leave their community, of married people who divorce, of neglected youth who are the children of divorced parents. You look at it all, and you understand that we can go only one step further than this. That one step is the denial of God.

Anybody who meets a person who has denied God becomes a contaminated person. He or she has to have great recourse to prayer and fasting in order to overcome the same temptation. But we forget these powerful remedies. We, too, laugh a strident laugh between two cocktails or amidst the sins of the flesh.

We laugh and we say, if only by our actions, "There isn't any God." Those of us who do this and yet call ourselves Christians and profess to believe in God, we really seduce mankind. That's the way we Catholics especially crucify the Lord Jesus Christ with hammer and nails. That's not doubt. That's giving in to the temptation of Satan himself. This has to be exorcised by fasting, prayer, and total obedience to a spiritual director.

Jesus Christ was obedient to his Father unto death. Now it is time for us to be obedient to death.

Be Christian on the Inside

Doubts come quickly, but the temptations of the evil one are slow in coming, because they need time to mature in the heart. The most tragic picture is the so-called believing Catholic who goes to church on Sunday, to Confession perhaps once a month, who acts outwardly as if he or she were a Catholic, but inside is not. Such a person is worried about everything, especially profit; is preoccupied by greed and desire; is worried about what's going to happen to him or her tomorrow or the day after. He or she refuses to let God direct his or her actions.

This doesn't mean that one has to abdicate intelligence. No, but one's life must be directed by the wisdom of God. Yet most lives aren't, and that is the great temptation that sweeps the world these days.

We call ourselves Catholics, but we don't care about our style of living, sexually or otherwise. We take bribes, because "everybody does it, so why not me?" We climb on the shoulders of our brethren in order to reach one more little rung of power, and then we go to church.

The evil one is ever present in that sort of thing. These are not doubts, which are more or less natural to man; they are temptations, the goal of which is the denial and the rejection of God.

This is why today we see people walking, not as pilgrims but as zombies, looking for God who is right by their side. This is what we must show the world—the face of Christ, through all our temptations and all our doubts. We must show the face of God. For this we exist. It is a hard road, but we have to tread it.

If we continue our pilgrimage toward God, in God, with God, then the road, though it be a narrow path, smoothes out, and we enter into the heart of Christ.

Battered by Worldly "Theologians"

"Have nothing to do with godless philosophical discussions—they only lead further and further away from true religion. Talk of this kind spreads corruption like gangrene."

2 Timothy 2:16,17

Pray and Fast

Doubts again! A wind! The kind which doesn't exist on earth—a hellish wind.

A priest stands alone in the midst of his doubts. They lie around him as if they were paper scraps from a garbage can, until he is almost ankle deep in all the doubts which whirl about him. He struggles mightily against all these little papers upon which are written down the opinions of so many scholars and theologians. He struggles not only with his own personal doubts but with a barrage of winds and ideas which leave him reeling and exhausted.

He's exhausted. If he stands, it's only because he is too tired to fall down. He cannot move one foot in front of another. He is too tired. The hellish rain of bits of paper continues to fall around him. Now they are knee-high, and slowly they rise up to his breast. Tomorrow or the day after, they'll bury him, the bits of garbage paper. The world seems brown to him, because he passes through the desert. It kills all vegetation. The sun beats mercilessly upon his heart.

He prays. He fasts. He begins to overcome his doubts.

Another wind comes, and it is a gentle breeze that caresses his tired face and somehow gives him to drink and even to eat. Slowly the face of the priest rises and his mind begins to clear.

Sweep Out the Sanctuary of Your Heart

Someone hands him a broom, or is it a limb of a tree? He starts cleaning a spot around himself. He stands between two winds—the angry wind which tries to destroy him, and the gentle wind which pushes the other one away.

The priest awakes. He bends down and gets a handful of scraps of paper and begins to read the words that are written there. A strange peace returns to him. He realizes that he was standing in the hallways of hell.

These scraps of paper were written by him who always disguises himself. Each paper speaks of doubts of the existence of God. Doubts concerning Christ's human life. Doubts about his resurrection, suggestions that he died like everybody else and that his body rotted in the ground. Doubts about his crucifixion. Doubts about all the things the so-called new theologians would write to a priest.

Pieces of paper are scattered around at his feet, and each one of them spelled death to his spirit. The priest knows now that this is an attack on the Church. He knows now that this very transparency is a gift from God, so that he can see how some theologians twist things around.

The "freedom" that they offer to other priests is a false freedom, leading to death instead of life. And now the priest has shaken himself, like a dog shakes when he gets wet. Now the step of the priest is firm. He moves with the purpose of faith, of love, of hope toward a poor kind of a table. Now his doubts have vanished under the gentle wind.

Still the priest moves toward the poor table. There are two candles and a saucer that somebody left which can barely pass for a chalice. In a firm and clear voice, the priest says, "This is my Body. This is my Blood." He, then, holds onto the table, and a hand pierced with nails gives him some bread and the wine from the chalice. He sees the face and the arms of Christ. All is peaceful now. Even the whisper of the scraps of paper has ceased. The sky is clear.

The sun is shining, and the priest has put his head on the breast of God. There he finds all he has been looking for.

Doubts about Sticking to Our Commitments to Love Another

"I, the prisoner in the Lord, urge you therefore to lead a life worthy of the vocation to which you were called. With all humility and gentleness, and with patience, support each other in love. Take every care to preserve the unity of the Spirit by the peace that binds you together."

Ephesians 4:1–3

Commitment

How beautiful is a bride; how handsome a groom. The white of the bride connotes virginity. Two people are getting married. They are supposed to love each other exceedingly. That's why they are getting married, so that two loves might blend into one, two bodies become one.

Of course, there are doubts. There are always doubts about a vocation, or shall we call it a commitment. There is always a little doubt when one engages in a commitment for life. So groom and bride probably had their moments of doubt before they were married, but love, if it was love, overcame it.

After Making the Commitment

But time went on, and strangely enough, as in so many cases, doubts grew, which meant that trust was diminished. Suddenly those who were supposed to be one before God, (which of course they were, but didn't want to face) decided to separate.

The doubts multiplied. She didn't trust him; he didn't trust her. He didn't like the way she nagged; she didn't like the way he was absent all the time. Whatever the reasons, trust was dying.

Did you ever hear trust die? It dies in a strange way in the hearts of people. It curls up like a newborn child, and suddenly, it becomes smaller and smaller and smaller, and then, it disappears. Where? Who can tell? Where does trust go? He and she trusted one another when they stood before the priest, she all dressed in white, and he desirous to build a home with and through her. They trusted one another, so it seemed, and then, the trust vanished, and the doubts came.

These were not doubts like a priest's. No scraps of paper filled their house. Nothing. The house was still as it was before. But, slowly, on a strange wind, through the cracks of the house, doubts entered in. Not necessarily doubts about the fidelity of one another, although they were there too, but doubts about the commitment.

Men lay in their beds in the depths of the night and ask themselves. "What did I do? I committed myself 'until death do us part.' But that's impossible. It can't be done. I cannot live with this woman."

Or a woman thinks about the man in the depth of the night, that she cannot live with him.

But neither of them stops to pray and to ask God, "How does one really commit oneself totally in a total commitment?"

The doubts become real. In the dark of the night each doubted the other and both felt sure of their doubts. When men and women feel sure of their doubts, hell laughs, because doubts now begin to be expressed in biting, cold, tragic words, and cynicism is born. Eventually, doubts become feet which lead men and women to lawyers.

At that moment, charity weeps over the children who had been born in love and yet are rejected because of doubts. Everything becomes chaotic. Far away, the voice of Jesus resounds, "What God has united, human beings must not divide." (Matthew 19:6) But all this is forgotten, and divorce becomes a tool of him who has planted the seeds of doubt in the hearts of the man and the woman.

Jesus Is the Good Samaritan

The evil one laughs—it is so good to see them fall into this net. He fills the net with divorced couples and presents it to Jesus Christ as a net filled with a thousand fish, mocking what Christ told his apostles.

Human law allows the two who once loved, who once begot children of love, to be "free."

The second Person of the most Holy Trinity walked this earth, so did his Mother. Jesus Christ comes riding on a donkey and comes across a man who has been beaten by robbers. He picks him up and brings him to the inn. There is a moment in the life of man when he knows that he is wounded. God holds him in his arms. Maybe because of this, because of the inn, those who were once one flesh, one blood, will come back again together.

So when God bends down to the man beaten up by robbers, hope springs in the heart of those who love God. And prayer ascends like a dove into the hands of the Father.

Let God bind your wounds. Let hope spring in your heart. Let your prayer ascend like a dove into the hands of the Father.

Living in the Modern Age

"Did you not know? Had you not heard?
Yahweh is the everlasting God,
he created the remotest parts of the earth.
He does not grow tired or weary,
his understanding is beyond fathoming.
He gives strength to the weary,
he strengthens the powerless.
Youths grow tired and weary,
the young stumble and fall,
but those who hope in Yahweh
will regain their strength,
they will sprout wings like eagles.
Though they run
they will not grow weary,
though they walk they will never tire."

Isaiah 40:28–31

Modern Doubts Sneak into Our Minds

Doubts have begun to march like armies, armies that are so dense that you can barely distinguish one soldier from another, especially in the twilight zone in which doubts walk these days. Political doubts. Spiritual doubts. Intellectual doubts.

An army marches shoulder to shoulder; men and women in the world are lost in that army of doubts. Never before has hell sent such an army. This army moves stealthily. It sneaks into the mind. Before one realizes it, one is invaded by this army of doubts.

"What shall we do?" questions the mind. "Are we about to have a war?" "Should we be friends with the People's Republic of China?" A thousand political and intellectual doubts besiege human beings, whose restless sleep can make hell laugh.

Before the carnage of the mind and the heart, a chasm opens. For the army desires to attack on one point, and one point only: "I give you a new commandment: love one another; you must love one another just as I have loved you." (John 13: 34) The voice comes from everywhere, and for a moment, the doubts are stilled, but only for a moment, because we realize that we do not love one another. Nation is pitted against nation, and the only thing that rules the world today is greed. Communism is just another form of greed.

Search for the Heart of the Trinity

It is a strange army that slowly penetrates the mind's ramparts and finally reaches its goal. Doubts about the political wisdom of nations is deeply embedded in the hearts of people. It's no use saying that the Russians have no doubts about their government. They do. Some nations are ready to translate doubts into fratricidal wars.

Doubts seem to rule everyone. But every person who believes in Christ knows deep down in his or her heart that doubts persist because he or she has set aside God in his or her life. God does not rule the nations any more, or so people like to think. That's why the scientists themselves don't know what is what. They come to the conclusion that there *might* be a God who has created this universe, but the scientific world is filled with "maybe" and "perhaps"—words of doubt.

Children look at their parents and hope that their parents are sure of something, someone, that they have no doubts about the fundamentals of life, especially, God. But parents are indifferent. They are occupied with themselves. Moreover, millions of children are children of divorced parents.

Where is escape? Where is a place, a spot, where doubts will fall asleep forever? There is only one place where man can find peace and the absence of doubts—in the heart of the Trinity.

Seek the heart of God.

Trust Jesus

"Consider it a great joy when trials of many kinds come upon you, for you well know that the testing of your faith produces perseverance, and perseverance must complete its work so that you will become fully developed, complete, not deficient in any way... Blessed is anyone who perseveres when trials come. Such a person is of proven worth and will win the prize of life, the crown that the Lord has promised to those who love him."

James 1:2–4,12

Doubts Are a Lack of Trust

So we really live amid doubts. They whirl around us like autumn leaves falling from the trees, making whispering sounds with each step we make. They encompass us, sometimes like a quiet rain, sometimes like a hurricane. They leave us rudderless, without oars in the middle of an unknown river. The trees along the shore seem to bend toward us as if they wanted to send doubts across the river.

Doubts encompass us all the time. Strange, isn't it, that we doubt so much. It comes down to this: doubts are a lack of trust. I might trust my husband or my wife, but then my imagination works overtime on his or her smallest faults. Doubt overcomes trust. When doubt overcomes trust, then love and hope shrivel up just like those autumn leaves that whisper under our feet. They become brown, dusty, dead.

Doubts Are Stepping Stones to God

Doubts are stepping stones to total trust in God and love of him.

But suppose we do not walk beyond those stepping stones? Suppose we pause somewhere in the middle and allow doubts to have their way. The Old Testament, the New Testament annoy us. We doubt everything pertaining to God. We fall into a general doubt. We doubt the authority that may interfere with our lives. In the twilight of a

gray day, we doubt ourselves and the purpose of our existence. These kinds of doubts
can lead people to jump off bridges in cities.

Depression

Then again, doubts might not lead to sui-
cide, but they do lead to depression, to all
kinds of emotional problems orchestrated by
the evil one. Emotional illnesses can completely spoil a human life, and they do so
because emotions have overcome faith. Once
the emotions overcome faith, then a lot of
things happen. Then the rustle of autumn
leaves under one's feet becomes like thunder
in one's ears. There is but one thing to do
when this happens, and that is to plunge
blindly into the waters of faith as Jesus did.
There is no other answer to those kinds of
doubts.

*Plunge into faith, into Jesus. Answer your doubts
by walking blindly in faith. Trust Jesus.*

Arise Again

"The people that walked in darkness
have seen a great light;
on the inhabitants of a country
in shadow dark as death
light has blazed forth...
Arise, shine out,
for your light has come,
and the glory of Yahweh has risen on you.
Look! Though night still covers the earth
and darkness the peoples,
on you Yahweh is rising
and over you his glory can be seen.
The nations will come to your light
and kings to your dawning brightness.
Lift up your eyes and look around:
all are assembling
and coming towards you."

Isaiah 9:1; 60:1–4

Faith Is a Gift

The other day, I was sitting with a priest who came to visit me on my island. It was one of those beautiful, cold, sunny days that Canada is so celebrated for. The river was a sheer, beautiful blanket of snow, tinted pink by the setting sun. The immense pines on the river's edges looked like a thousand pilgrims thronging around and about the river, hoping for a thaw, perhaps so they could drink of it.

The priest was talking about faith. Strangely enough, I had been meditating on faith. I suddenly turned to the priest and asked, "Why is it that I find it so difficult to communicate with Christians on this continent? There seems to be some sort of a curtain or wall between us. Yet I love them so terribly much. Why should this be?"

The priest, a Canadian, answered me quite simply, "Catherine, we are not a people of faith, in a manner of speaking. Oh, yes, we believe, but it is mostly with the head that we believe. For us faith has been, and often probably still is, a set of moral obligations.

"A Christian does such and such things—a Christian doesn't do such and such things. A priest does such and such things—a priest doesn't do such and such things. The same applies to monks and nuns."

Then, the priest had to leave.

I looked at the snowy expanse of the river, now tinged with the blue shadows of the evening, and cried out, "But faith is none of these things!"

Faith is a gift—a gift given by God to humanity. The Christian faith is received by a person when, through baptism, he is immersed in the death and resurrection of Jesus Christ. Faith is a pure gift. God alone can bestow it. And God desires passionately to give it to us.

I Believe, Lord, Help My Unbelief

Faith is assented to again and again. It is the *fiat* of a person, who, as he grows to maturity, continues to say, "Yes, I believe," and acts accordingly. "Acting accordingly" means that a person realizes that faith goes far beyond reason, that a person of faith folds the wings of his intellect, and in a strange manner, loses his "spiritual" eyesight and hearing and perhaps even becomes dumb, speechless.

Faith must go through this strange dark land, following him whom it loves. The Christian must arise at some point of his life, and go around and about in the darkness of the night asking whoever may be present, "Have you seen him whom I love?" Faith is a country of darkness in which one ventures because one *loves* and *believes* in the Beloved, God, the Father, the Son, and the Holy Spirit—who is above all reasoning, understanding, comprehension, and who, paradoxically, is at the same time enclosed within me.

Walking in darkness pits our peanut-brain against the mystery of faith. We want to tear apart the very thin veil of faith—to see if we can weigh it, measure it. When we ask, "What is faith?" we become, somehow, like ghosts, and faith always eludes us when we approach it this way.

The only way to approach faith is on our knees—through prayer. We should not only kneel, but we should prostrate ourselves before God—imploring—crying out for growth in faith, so that we may believe ever more firmly, not only in God, but also in man who is fashioned in God's image. Faith heals by asking God to heal.

Enter the Dark Night with the Hope of a Child

Faith is fundamentally a kind of folly, I guess—the folly that belongs to God himself, for "no eye has seen and no ear has heard... all that God has prepared for those who love him." (1 Corinthians 2:9) Faith, in all its folly, allows us to enter peacefully into the dark night which faces every one of us at one time or another.

Faith walks simply, childlike, between the darkness of human life and the hope of what is to come. Precariousness and finiteness are but the womb in which faith abides, moving towards the plenitude and fullness of the eternity that it desires and believes in, and that revelation opens to it.

Through faith, a person's face is turned to God, and their eyes meet. Then, every day becomes more and more luminous. The veil between God and you becomes less and less until it seems that you can almost reach out and touch God. Faith breaks through barriers. Faith makes love into a bonfire, and holds the wind of the Holy Spirit who fans the bonfire.

Those who set out on this quest for God, and enter this land of the strange and warm darkness, are the only ones who will have the power to save humanity in this hour of peril. If you are one of these, you may, for a time, be unable to hear—or to see—or even to speak. But in an instant, you will be mysteriously visited.

A hand will touch your ears and they will be opened, not only to the speech of man but to the speech of God.

A hand will touch your eyes and you will see, not only with the eyes of man but with the sight of God.

A hand will touch your tongue and you will speak, not only as man speaks but as God speaks, and you will have become a prophet of the Lord.

Along the road of this darkness of faith, people fall, people sin—but always, always they arise again.

Kneel. Prostrate yourself. Cry out to God for faith. Proclaim your fiat, "Yes, I believe." Then, arise. Arise again and go. Go into the dark night with love and with hope. Go as a pilgrim to the light of faith. Live the gift of faith that God alone bestows.

Afterword

Jesus said, "Whoever acknowledges me before men, I will acknowledge before my Father." Now is the hour. Doubts fall away, and Christ is acknowledged by men, women, and children. Now faith has spread its wings and chased away all doubts. This is the moment of joy. It doesn't matter that it might be also the moment of pain.

St. Peter says to us, "This is a great joy to you, even though for a short time yet you must bear all sorts of trials; so that the worth of your faith, more valuable than gold, which is perishable even if it has been tested by fire, may be proved—to your praise and honour when Jesus Christ is revealed. You have not seen him, yet you love him; and still without seeing him you believe in him and so are already filled with a joy so glorious that it cannot be described; and you are sure of the goal of your faith, that is, the salvation of your souls." (1 Peter 1:6–9)

Joy overcomes pain, because now we suddenly know that all the while we were in darkness, knocking at all kinds of doors,

Christ was there. So we stopped knocking and fell prostrate before his face. Somehow we knew that he would come to us, and he did. Those who shed their doubts through faith know the resurrection. It is only when we really doubt, and things are in the twilight zone, that we realize what the resurrection is.

Christ rose on the third day. Because he did, I have no doubts. Nor should you have any, for the simple reason that, obedient to his Father, Christ came to us, the sign of reconciliation under the sign of the cross. He died for us, and was buried for us, and then, on the third day, he arose. When faith conquers, doubts disappear. Alleluia! Alleluia! Alleluia!

MADONNA HOUSE PUBLICATIONS
COMBERMERE • ONTARIO • CANADA • K0J 1L0

"Lord, give bread to the hungry, and hunger for you to those who have bread," was a favourite prayer of our foundress, Catherine Doherty. At Madonna House Publications, we strive to satisfy the spiritual hunger for God in our modern world with the timeless words of the Gospel message.

Faithful to the teachings of the Catholic Church and its magisterium, Madonna House Publications is a non-profit apostolate dedicated to publishing high quality and easily accessible books, audiobooks, videos and music. We pray our publications will awaken and deepen in our readers an experience of Jesus' love in the most simple and ordinary facets of everyday life.

Your generosity can help Madonna House Publications provide the poor around the world with editions of important spiritual works containing the enduring wisdom of the Gospel message. If you would like to help, please send your contribution to the address below. We also welcome your questions and comments. May God bless you for your participation in this apostolate.

Madonna House Publications
2888 Dafoe Rd
Combermere ON   K0J 1L0
Canada

Internet: www.madonnahouse.org/publications

E-mail: publications@madonnahouse.org

Telephone: (613) 756-3728